BOOKS IN THIS SERIES

Draw 50 Airplanes, Aircraft, and Spacecraft
Draw 50 Animals
Draw 50 Athletes
Draw 50 Beasties and Yugglies and Turnover Uglies and Things That Go
               Bump in the Night
Draw 50 Boats, Ships, Trucks, and Trains
Draw 50 Buildings and Other Structures
Draw 50 Cars, Trucks, and Motorcycles
Draw 50 Cats
Draw 50 Creepy Crawlies
Draw 50 Dinosaurs and Other Prehistoric Animals
Draw 50 Dogs
Draw 50 Endangered Animals
Draw 50 Famous Caricatures
Draw 50 Famous Cartoons
Draw 50 Famous Faces
Draw 50 Flowers, Trees, and Other Plants
Draw 50 Holiday Decorations
Draw 50 Horses
Draw 50 Monsters, Creeps, Superheroes, Demons, Dragons, Nerds, Dirts,
               Ghouls, Giants, Vampires, Zombies, and Other Curiosa . . .
Draw 50 People
Draw 50 People of the Bible
Draw 50 Sharks, Whales, and Other Sea Creatures
Draw 50 Vehicles

DRAW 50 CARS, TRUCKS, AND MOTOR- CYCLES

DRAW 50 CARS, TRUCKS, AND MOTOR- CYCLES

Lee J. Ames

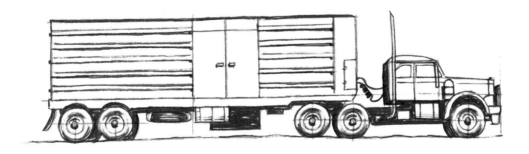

DOUBLEDAY
NEW YORK   LONDON   TORONTO   SYDNEY   AUCKLAND

A MAIN STREET BOOK
PUBLISHED BY DOUBLEDAY
a division of Bantam Doubleday Dell Publishing Group, Inc.
1540 Broadway, New York, New York 10036

MAIN STREET BOOKS, DOUBLEDAY, and the portrayal of a
building with a tree are trademarks of Doubleday, a
division of Bantam Doubleday Dell Publishing Group, Inc.

Library of Congress Cataloging-in-Publication Data:
Ames, Lee J.
    Draw 50 cars, trucks, and motorcycles.
    Summary: Provides step-by-step instructions on how to draw a variety of cars,
trucks, and motorcycles, including a Ford Thunderbird, cement trucks, and minibikes.
    1. Motor vehicles in art—Juvenile literature.   2. Drawing—Technique—Juvenile
literature.   [1. Motor vehicles in art.   2. Drawing—Technique]   I. Title.   II. Title:
Draw fifty cars.
NC825.M64A44   1986   743'.896292   85-13157
ISBN 0-385-19059-X
ISBN 0-385-19060-3(lib. bdg.)
ISBN 0-385-24639-0 (pbk.)

To Mark David and Hillary Leigh, my two grand kids!

. . . and thanks to Warren Budd for all his help.

TO THE READER

This book will show you a way to draw cars, trucks, bikes and motorcycles. You need not start with the first illustration. Choose whichever you wish. When you have decided, follow the step-by-step method shown. *Very lightly* and *carefully*, sketch out step number one. However, this step, which is the easiest, should be done *most carefully*. Step number two is added right to step number one, also lightly and also very carefully. Step number three is sketched right on top of numbers one and two. Continue this way to the last step.

It may seem strange to ask you to be extra careful when you are drawing what seem to be the easiest first steps, but this is most important because a careless mistake at the beginning may spoil the whole picture at the end. As you sketch out each step, watch the spaces between the lines, as well as the lines, and see that they are the same. After each step, you may want to lighten your work by pressing it with a kneaded eraser (available at art supply stores).

When you have finished, you may want to redo the final step in India ink with a fine brush or pen. When the ink is dry, use the kneaded eraser to clean off the pencil lines. The eraser will not affect the India ink.

Here are some suggestions: In the first few steps, even when all seems quite correct, you might do well to hold your work up to a mirror. Sometimes the mirror shows that you've twisted the drawing off to one side without being aware of it. At first you may find it difficult to draw the boxes, triangles, or circles, or just to make the pencil go where you wish. Don't be discouraged. The more you practice, the more control you will develop. Use a compass or a ruler if you wish; professional artists do! The only equipment you'll need will be a medium or soft pencil, paper, the kneaded eraser and, if you wish, a compass, ruler, pen, or brush.

The first steps in this book are shown darker than necessary so that they can be clearly seen. (Keep your own work very light.)

Remember, there are many other ways and methods to make drawings. This book shows just one method. Why don't you seek out other ways and methods to make drawings— from teachers, from libraries and, most importantly . . . from inside yourself?

LEE J. AMES

SPECIAL NOTES:

On drawing wheels:
Since many of the wheels in this book are angled and not perfect circles, I've used a "drawn from quartering" method to achieve the appropriate roundness.

"Faking":
When drawing complex motor or machinery detail, if you were to include every nut, bolt, spring, cylinder etc., it would take forever and distract you from being concerned with the whole picture. "Faking" is one solution. "Faking" is drawing in the general look of something as complex as an engine with strong strokes, dashes, dots, squiggles etc. that just suggest the subject. See below:

TO THE PARENT OR TEACHER

"Leslie can draw a Rolls-Royce better than anybody else!" Such peer acclaim and encouragement generate incentive. Contemporary methods of art instruction (freedom of expression, experimentation, self-evaluation of competence and growth) provide a vigorous, fresh-air approach for which we must all be grateful.

New ideas need not, however, totally exclude the old. One such is the "follow me, step-by-step" approach. In my young learning days this method was so common, and frequently so exclusive, that the student became nothing more than a pantographic extension of the teacher. In those days it was excessively overworked.

This does not mean that the young hand is never to be guided. Rather, specific guiding is fundamental. Step-by-step guiding that produces satisfactory results is valuable even when the means of accomplishment are not fully understood by the student.

The novice with a musical instrument is frequently taught to play simple melodies as quickly as possible, well before he learns the most elemental scratchings at the surface of music theory. The resultant self-satisfaction, pride in accomplishment, can be a significant means of providing motivation. And all from mimicking an instructor's "Do-as-I-do . . ."

Mimicry is prerequisite for developing creativity. We learn the use of our tools by mimicry. Then we can use those tools for creativity. To this end I would offer the budding artist the opportunity to memorize or mimic (rote-like, if you wish) the making of "pictures." "Pictures" he has been anxious to be able to draw.

The use of this book should be available to anyone who *wants* to try another way of flapping his wings. Perhaps he or she will then get off the ground when a friend says, "Leslie can draw a Rolls-Royce better than anybody else!"

LEE J. AMES

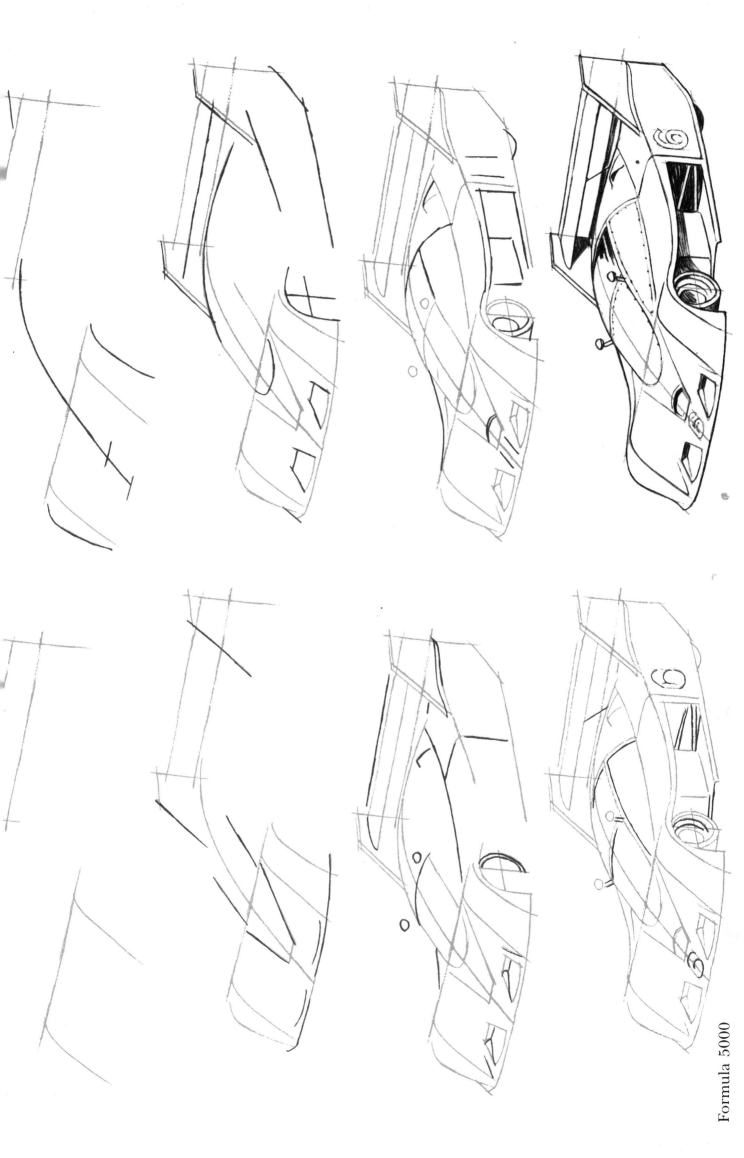

Formula 5000

Jaguar XK-E 2+2 4.2 litre

Gabelich's "Blue Flame"—1970

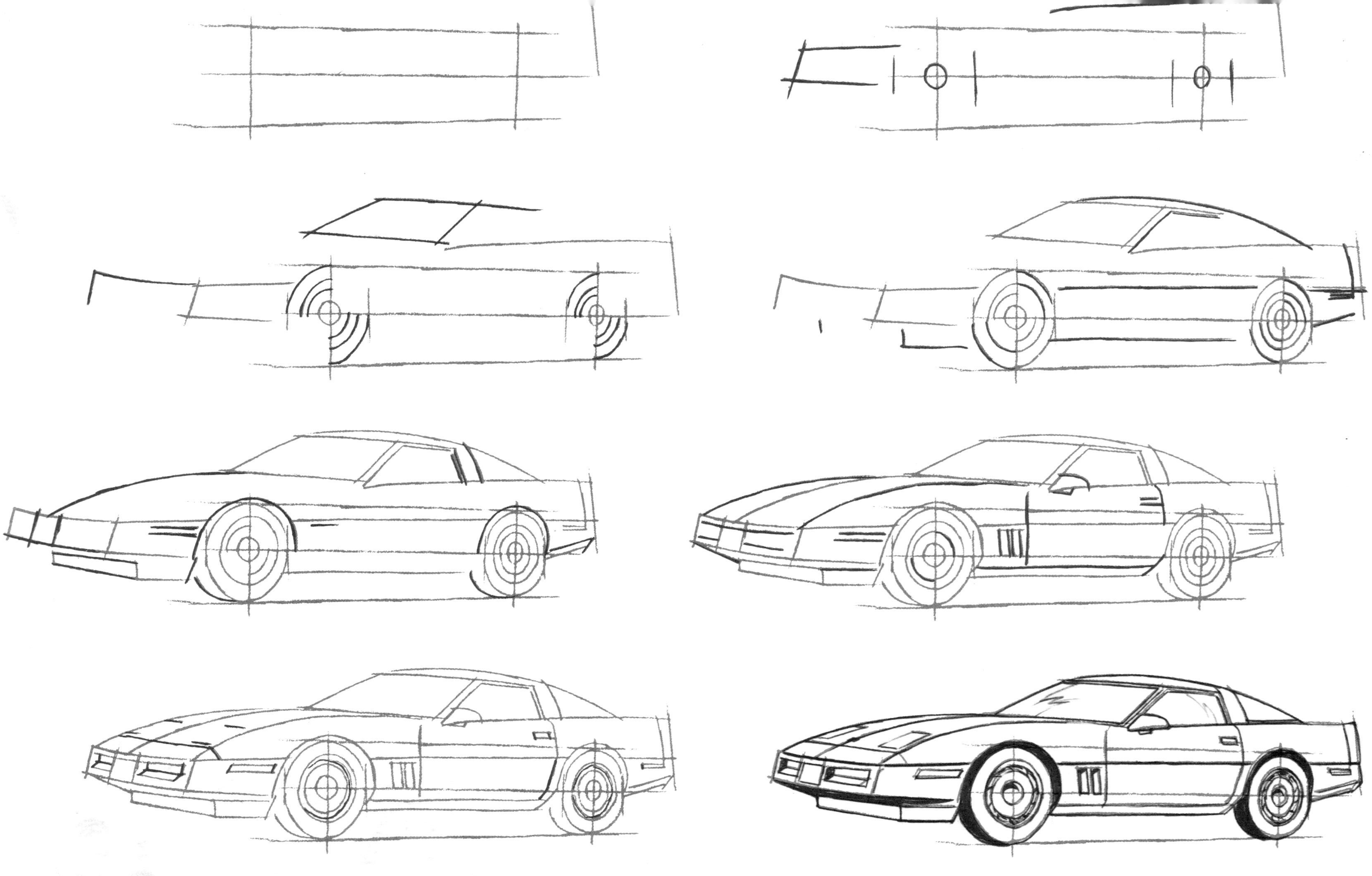

1984 Chevrolet Corvette

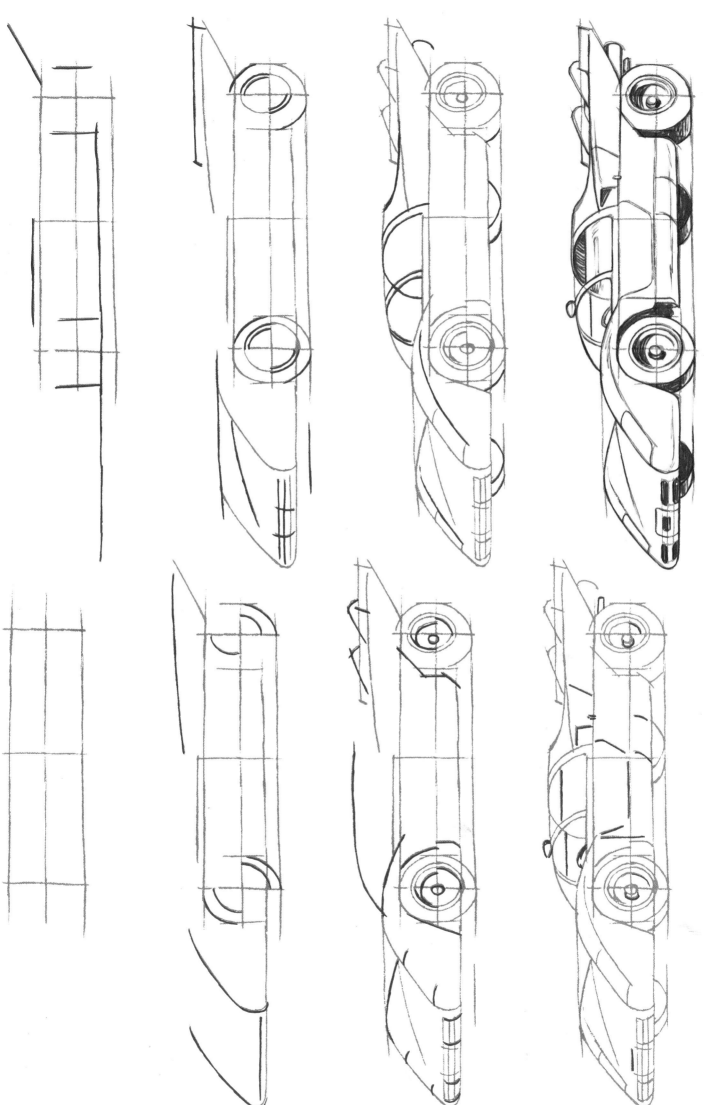

Ferrari 512S Racer

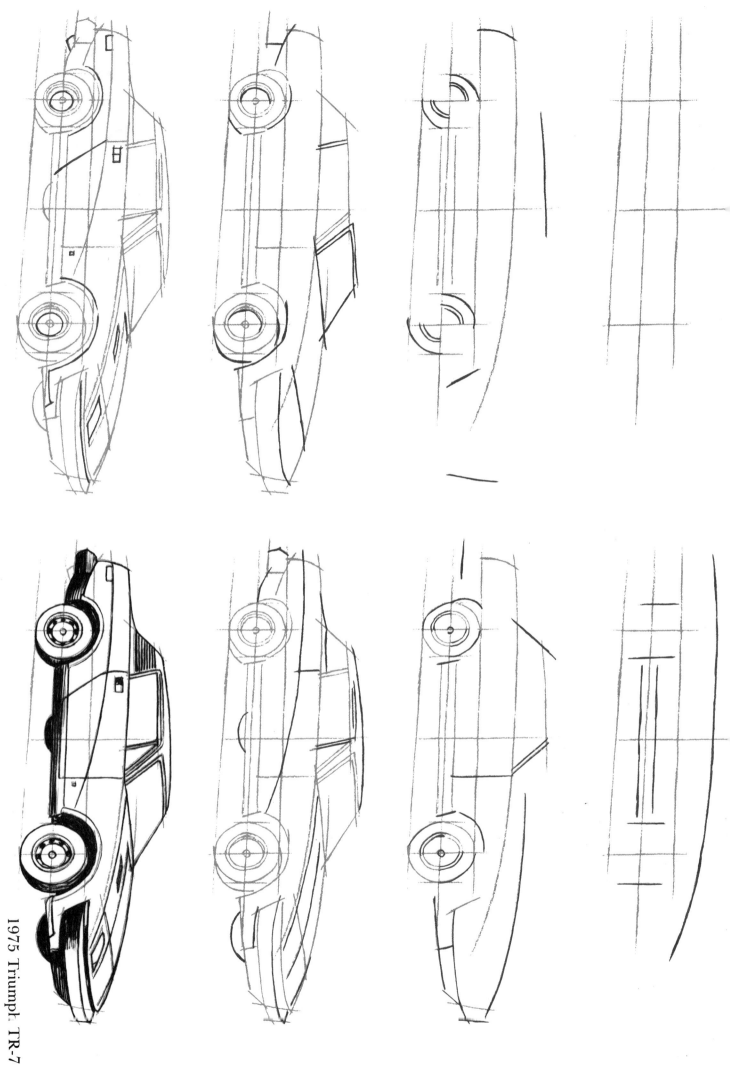

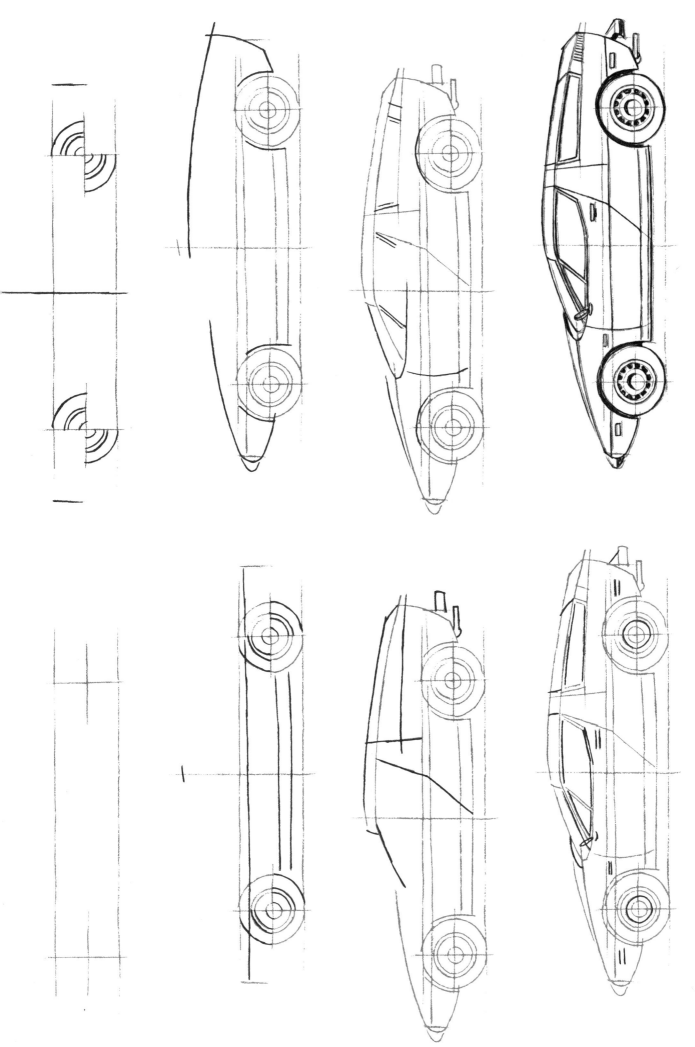

1977 Maserati Bora

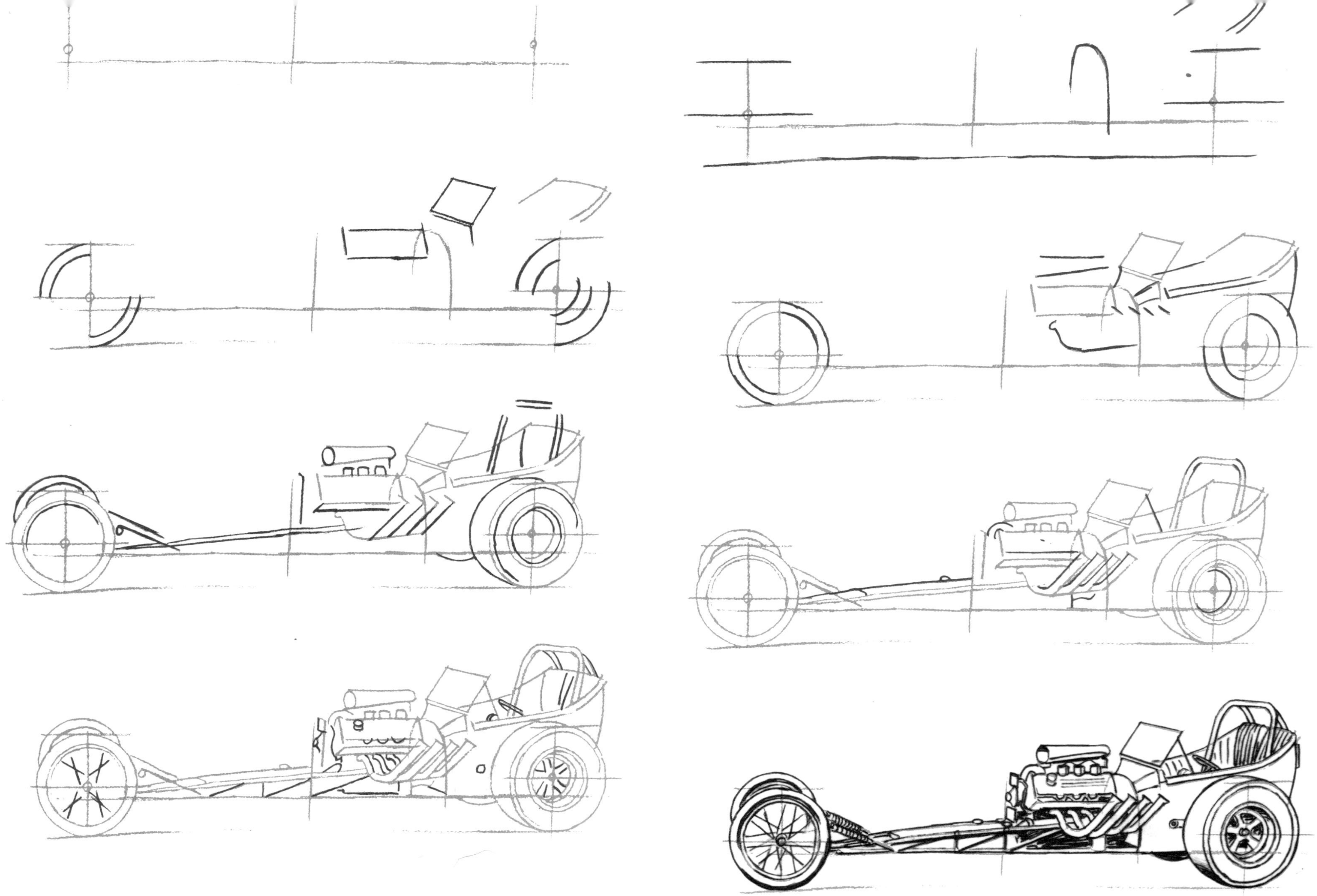

Dragster—1967 Ford

Hot Rod

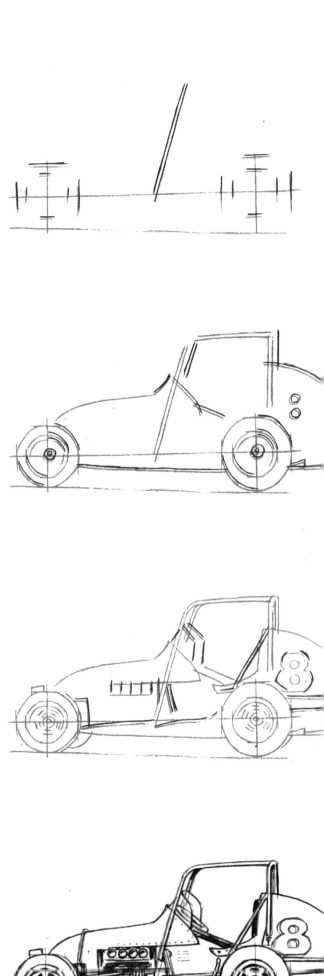

USAC Midget

Hot Rod—Gary Reymund's '23

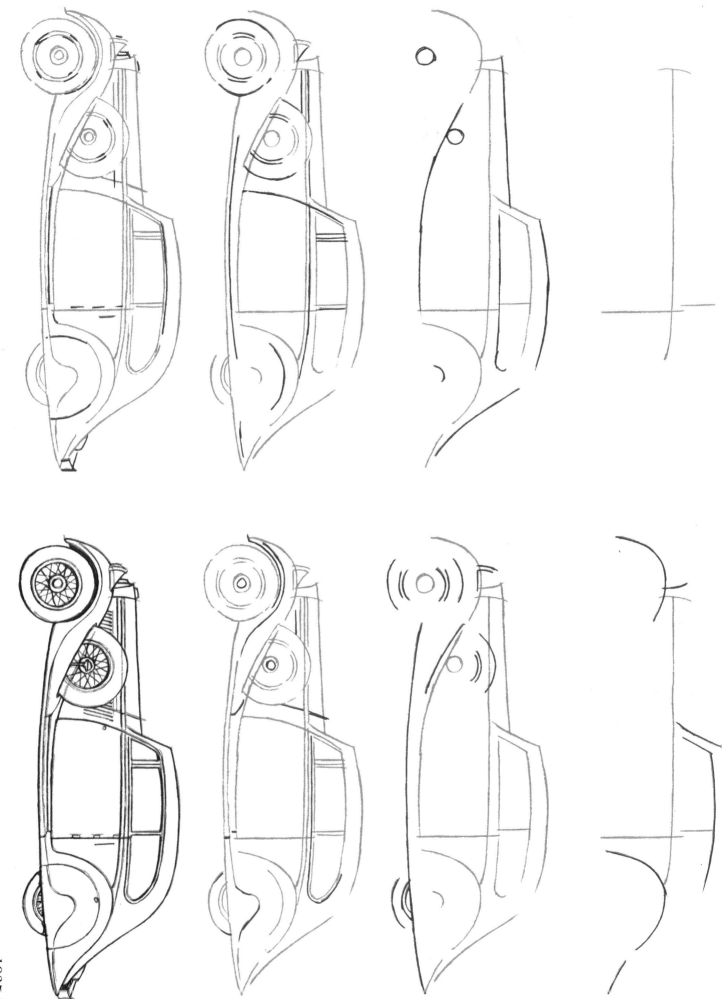

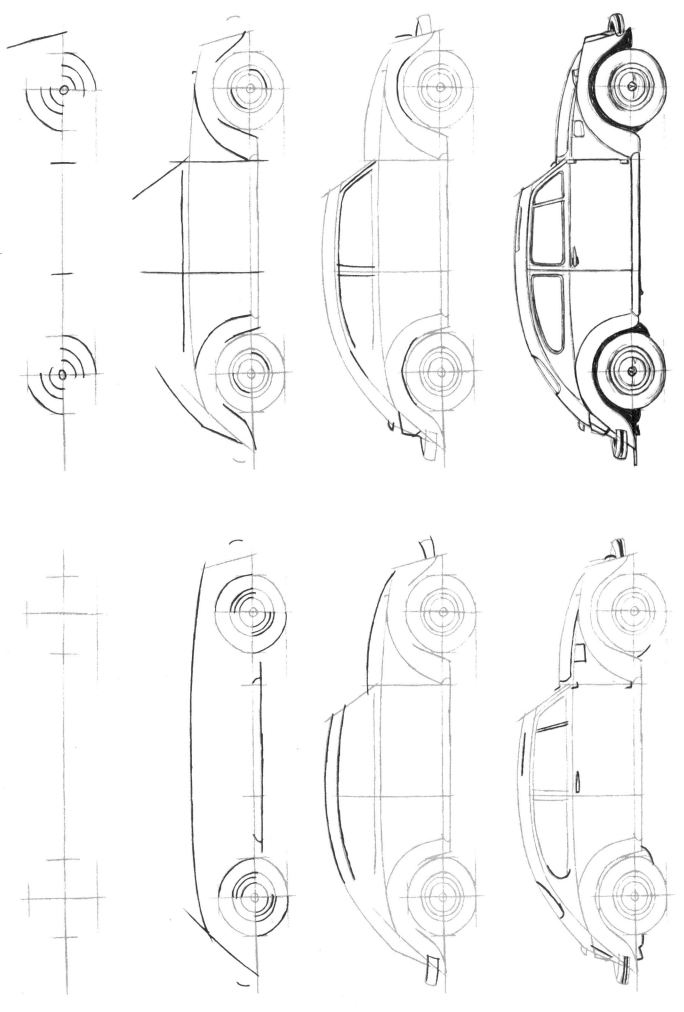

1974 Volkswagen Beetle

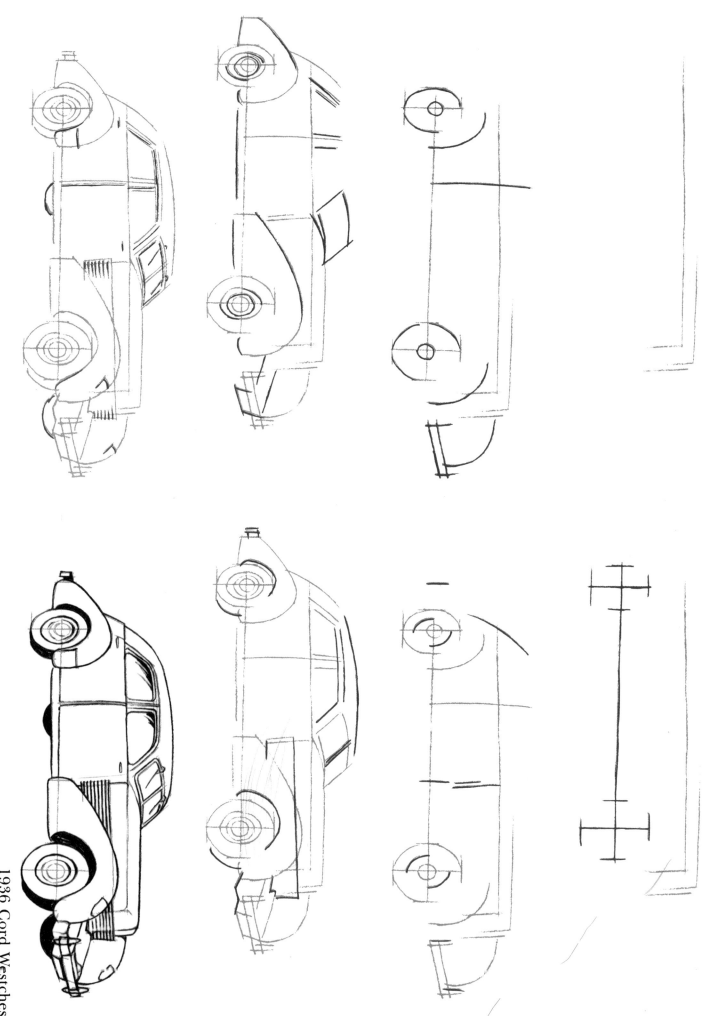

1936 Cord Westchester

1936 Bugatti Surbaisse

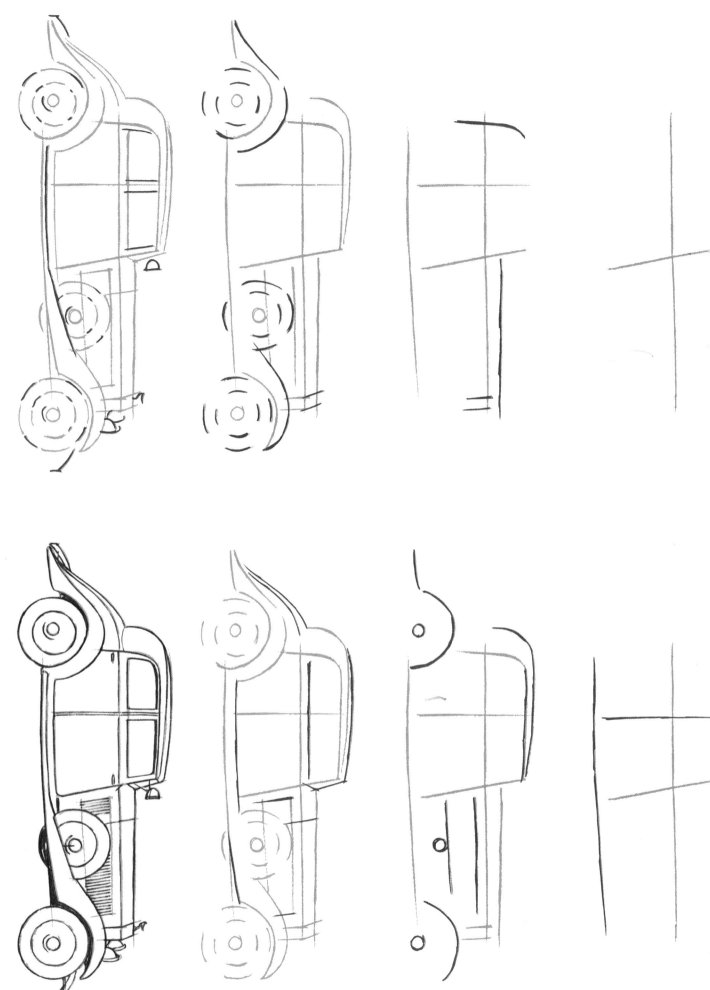

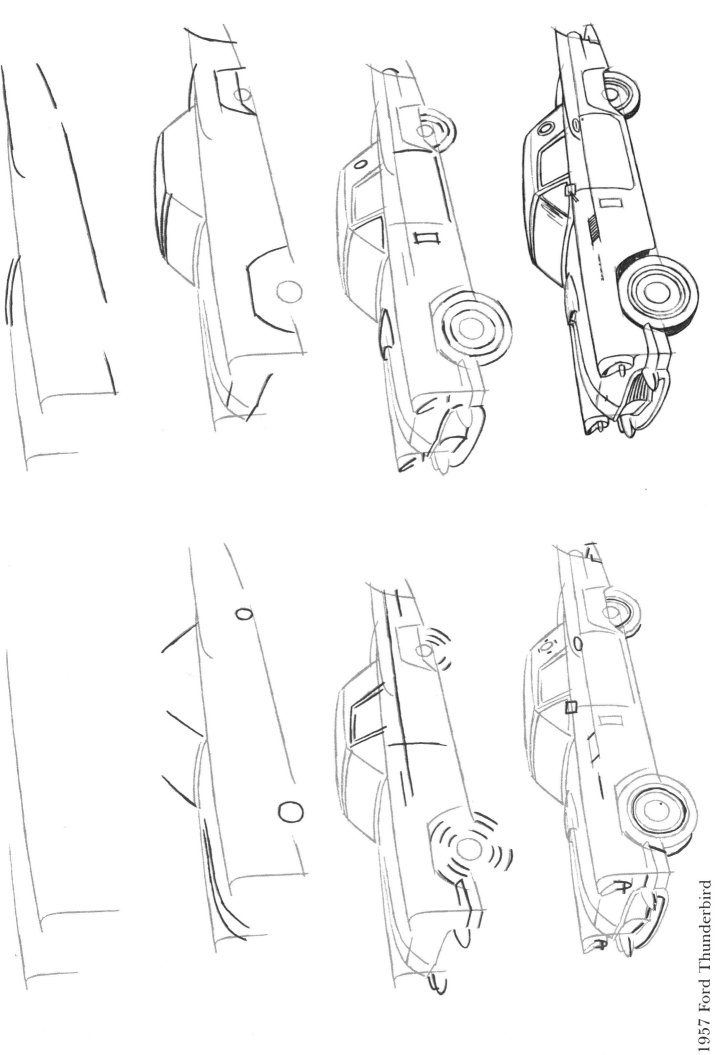

1957 Ford Thunderbird

1912 Brewster Town Car

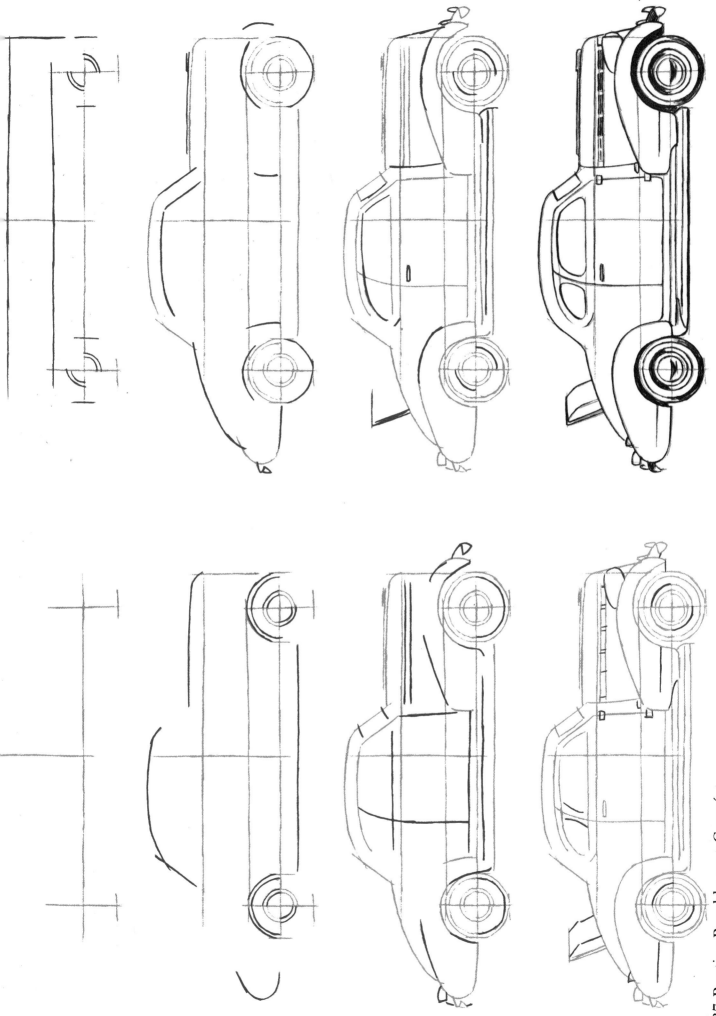

1937 Pontiac Rumble-seat Coupé

1974 Glassic Model A replica

1964 Ford Mustang

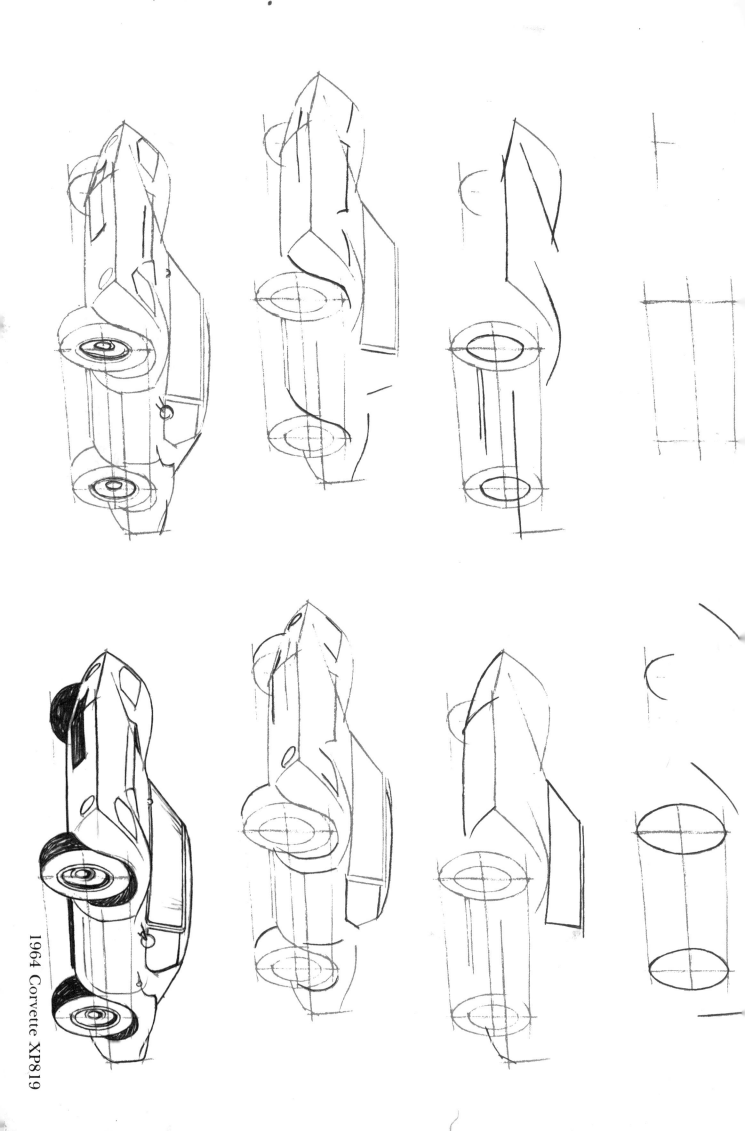

1964 Corvette XP819

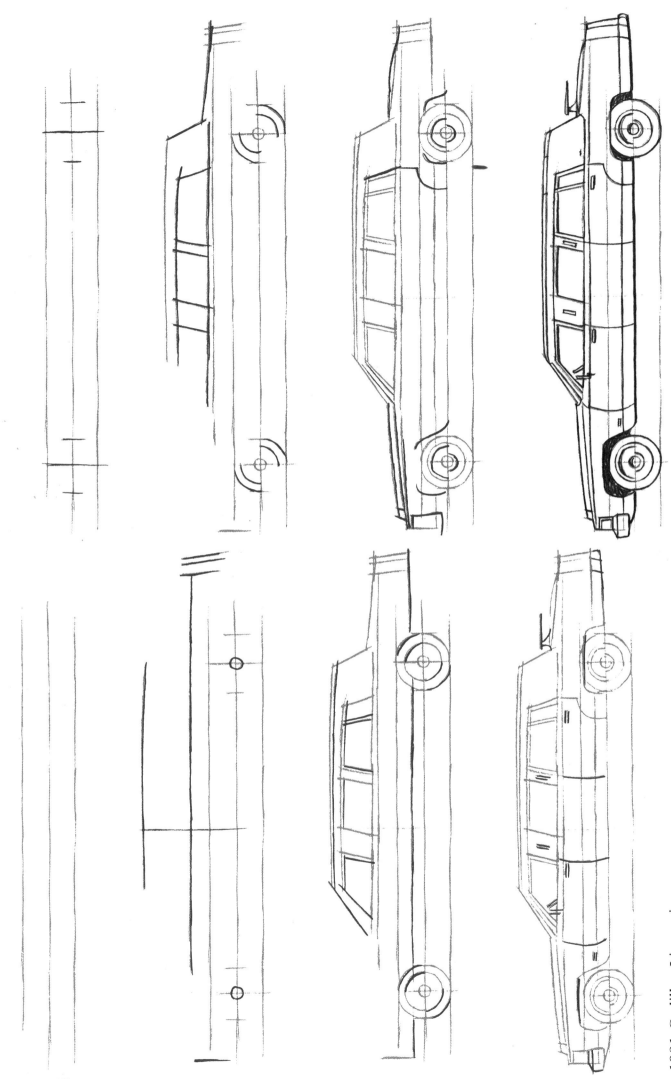

1981 Cadillac Limousine

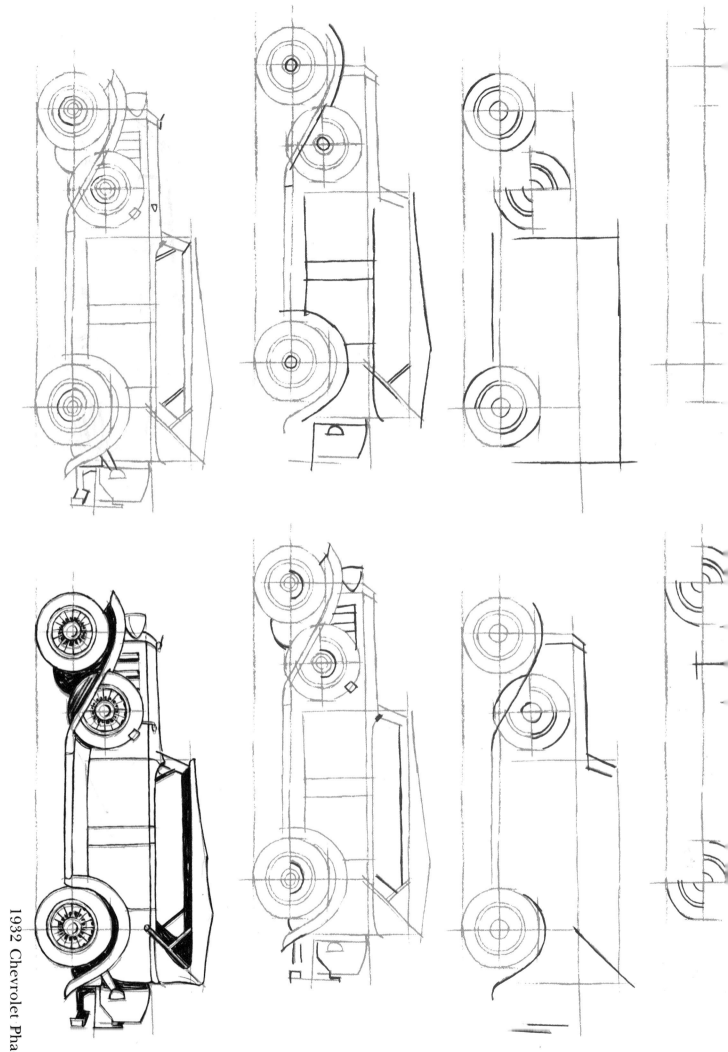

1932 Chevrolet Phaeton

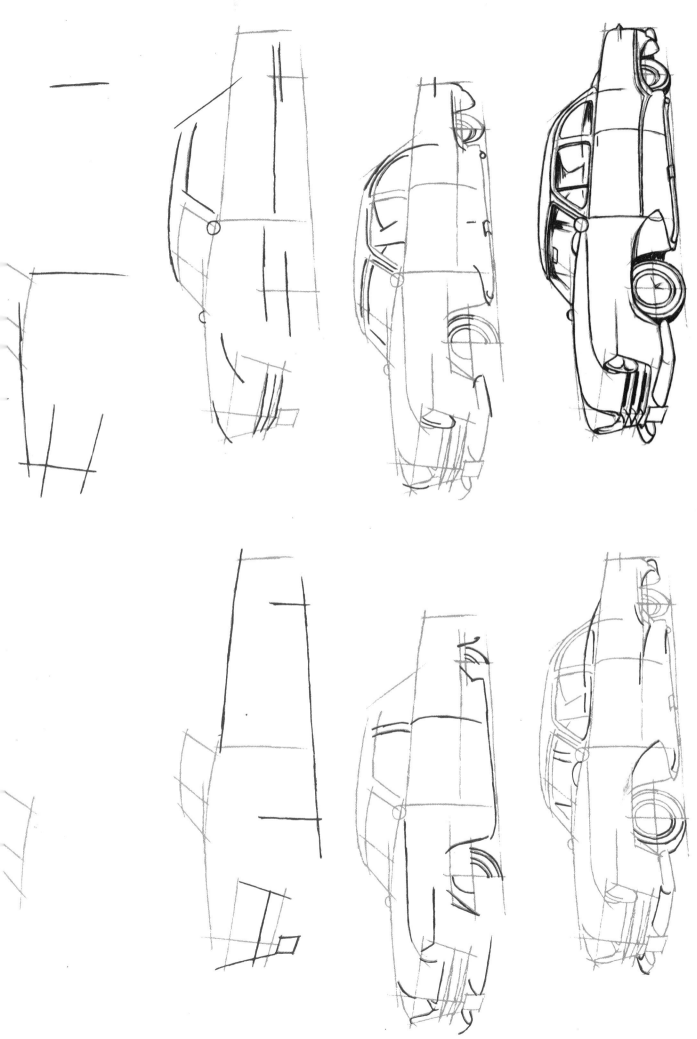

Modified 1951 Ford—low rider

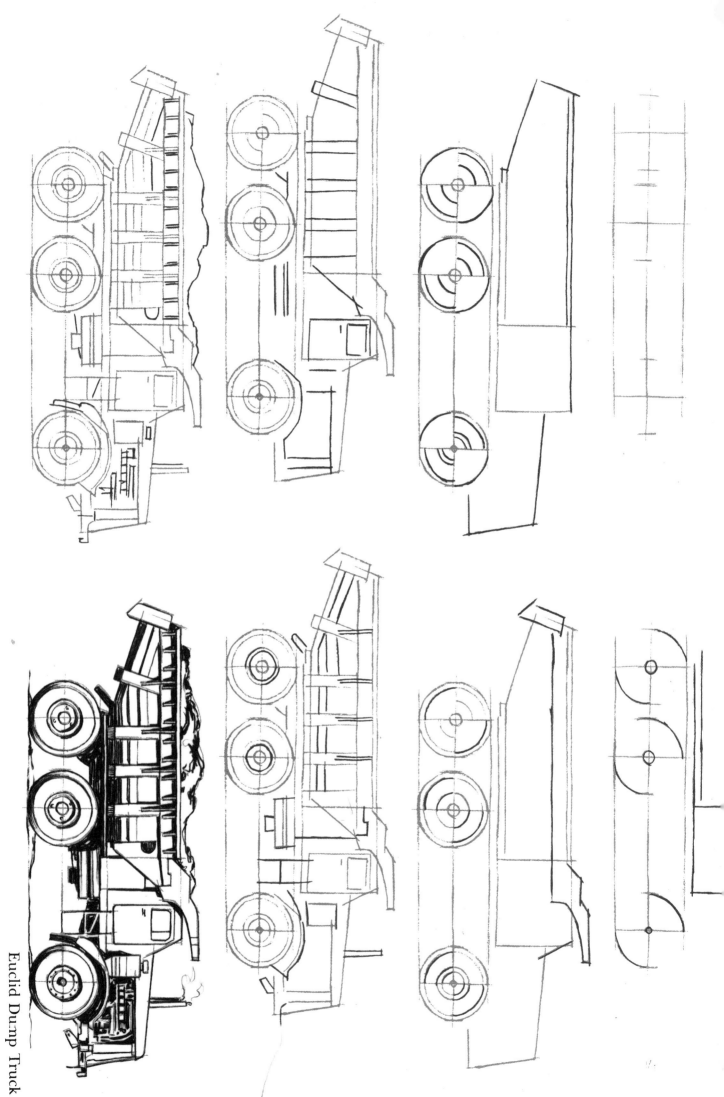

Euclid Dump Truck

Refrigerator Trailer

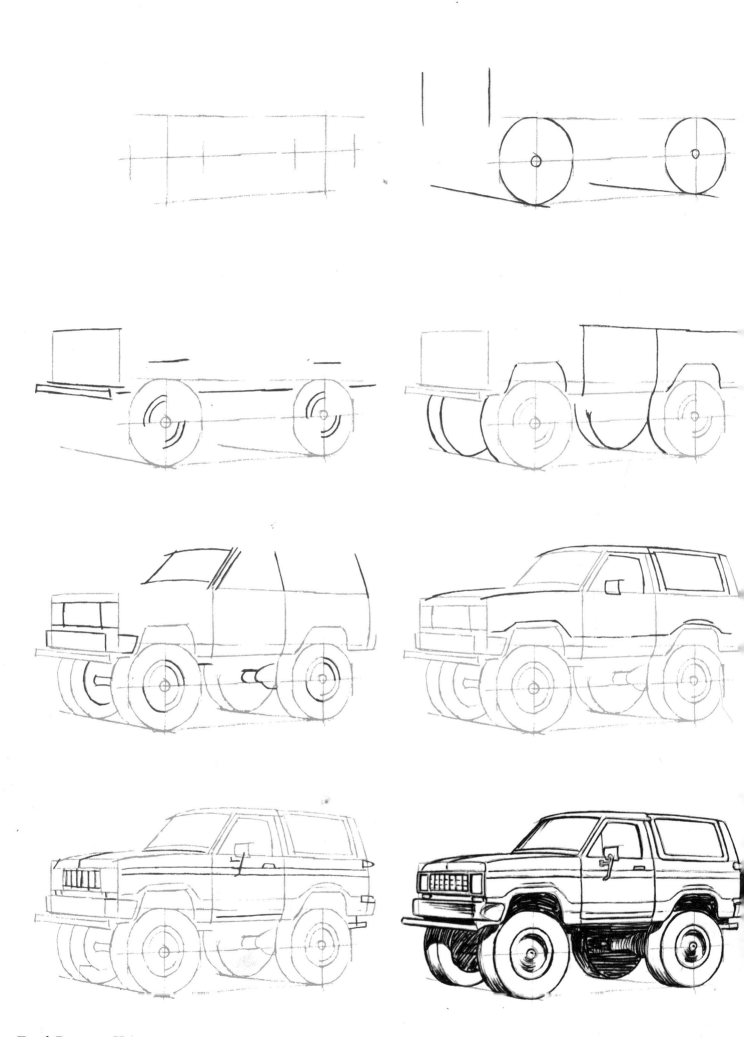

Ford Bronco II

1974 Ford E-100 Custom Van

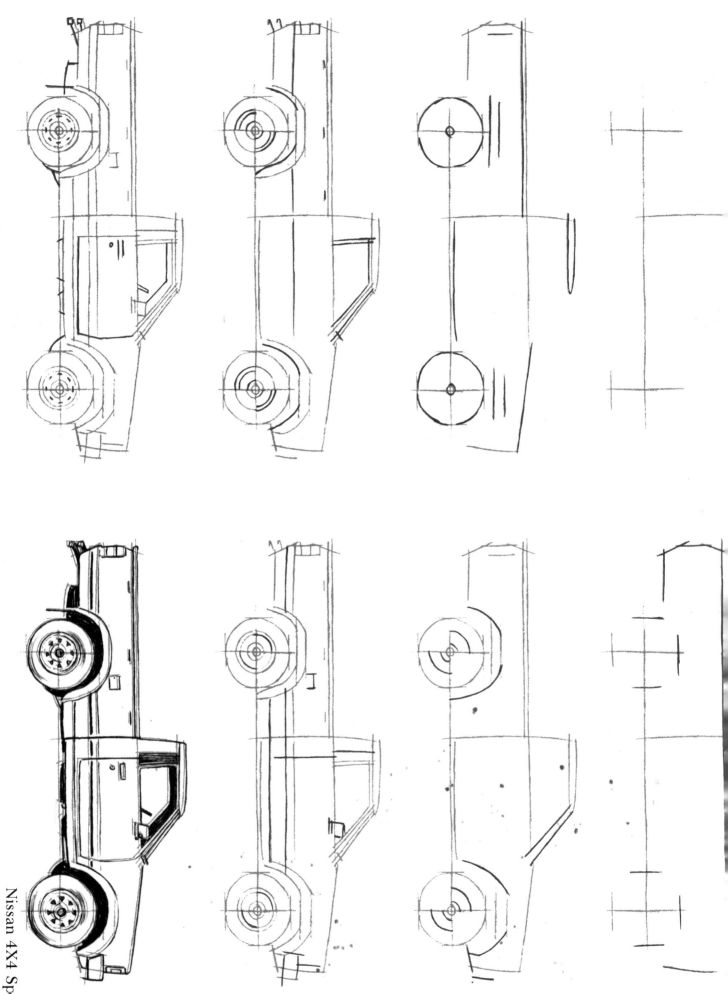

Nissan 4X4 Sport Truck

Mazda B2000 Sundowner

Micro Van—Subaru's Domingo

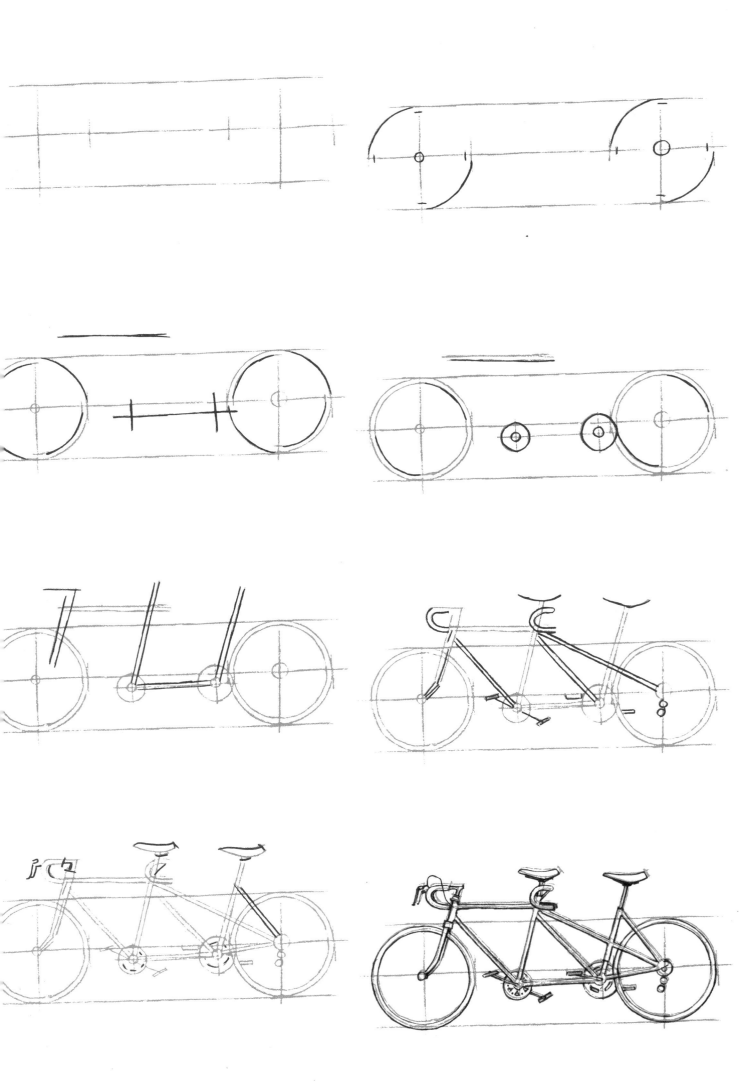

Tandem Bicycle

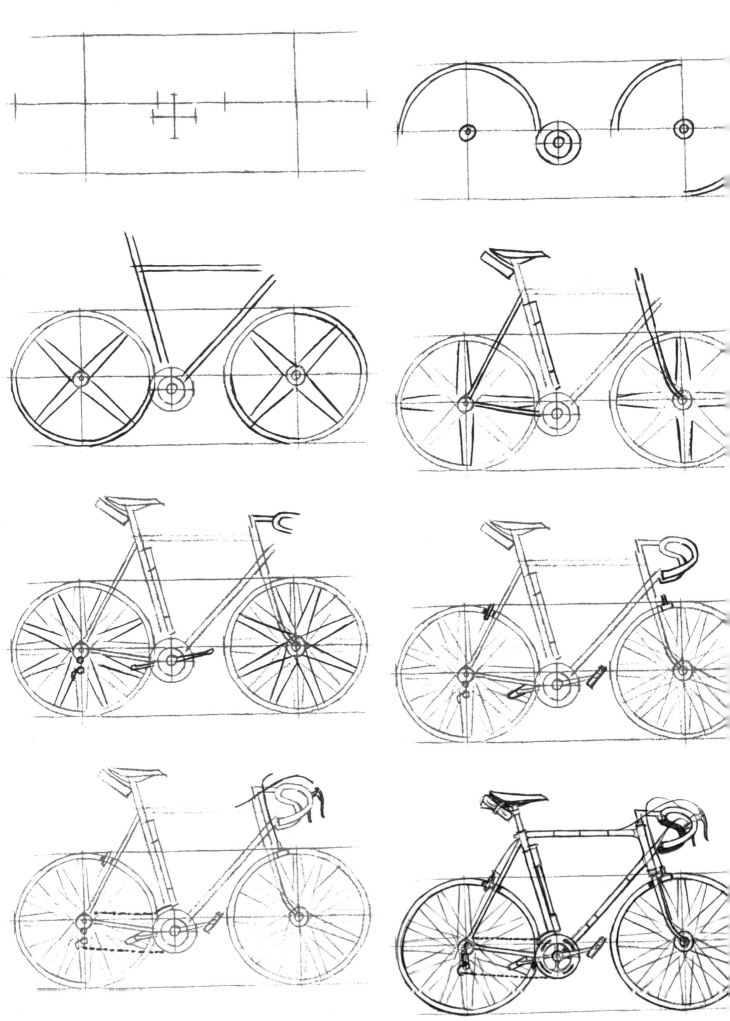

Road Racing Superbike

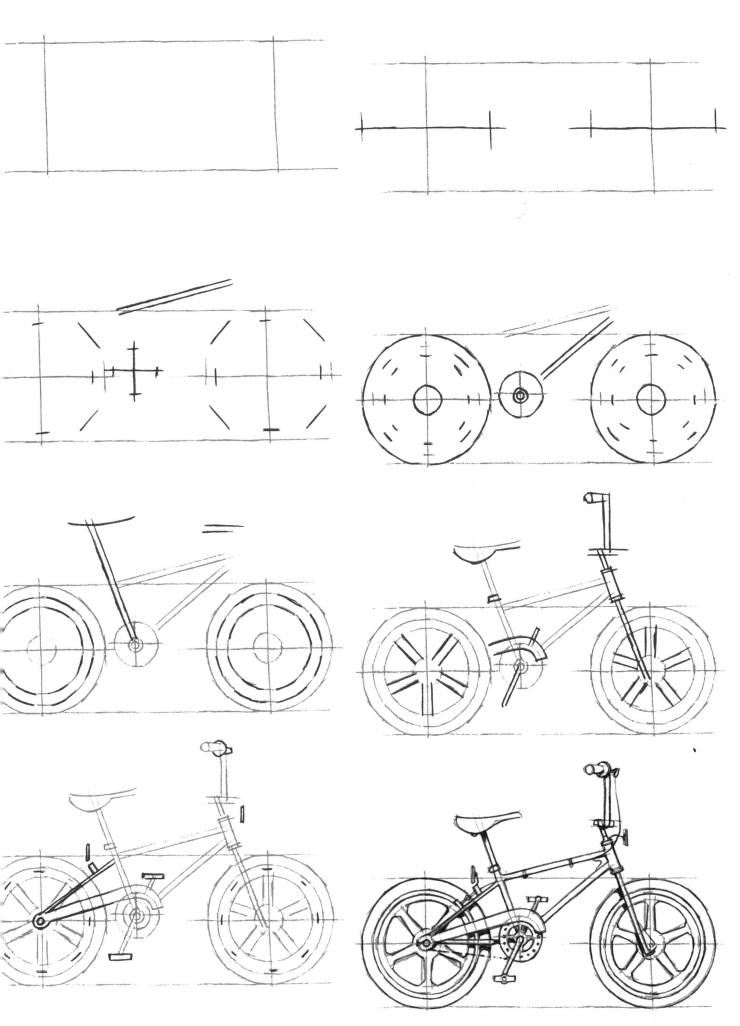

Motocross (Panasonic) with Piranha wheels

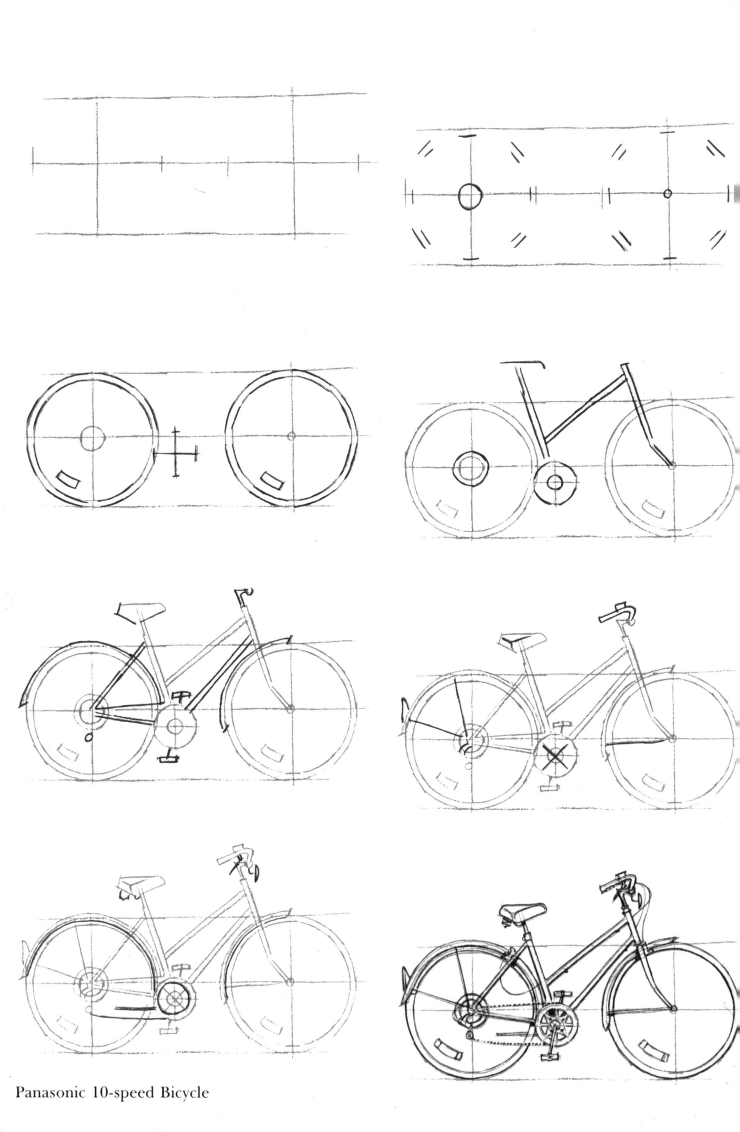

Panasonic 10-speed Bicycle

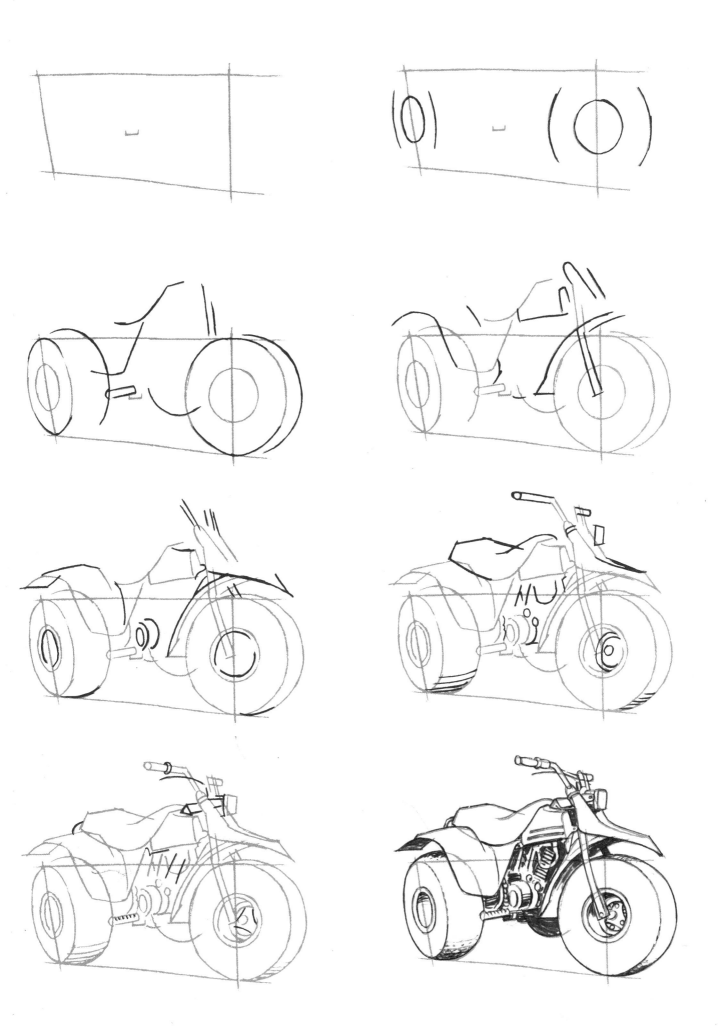

Suzuki ALT 125 3X6

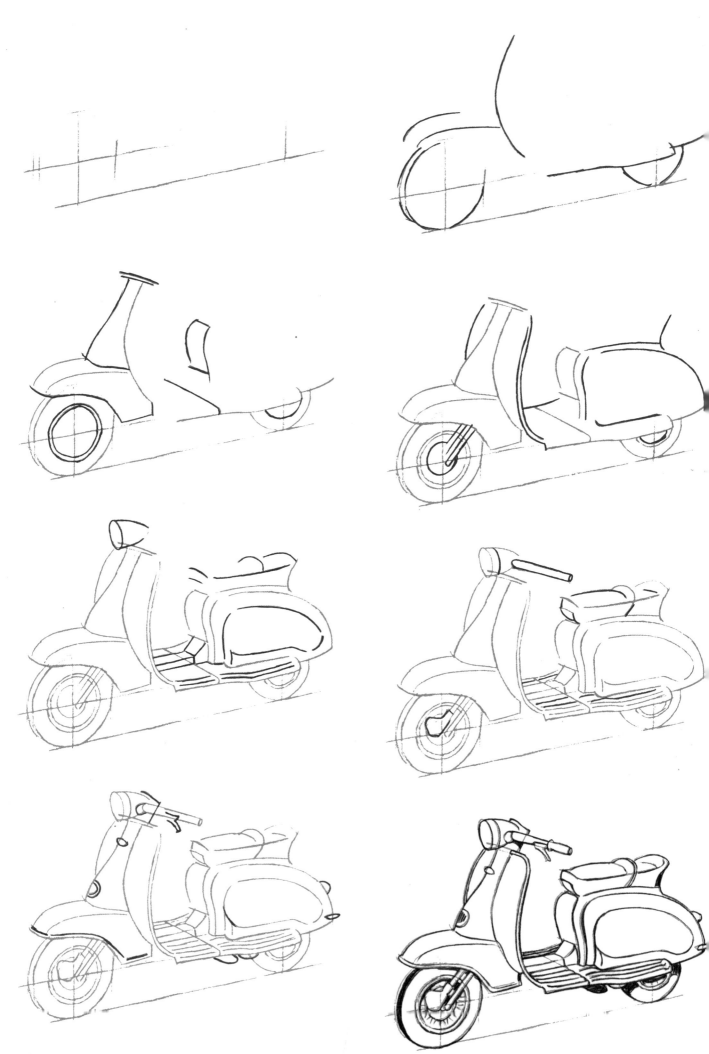

Lambretta Scooter T-V175

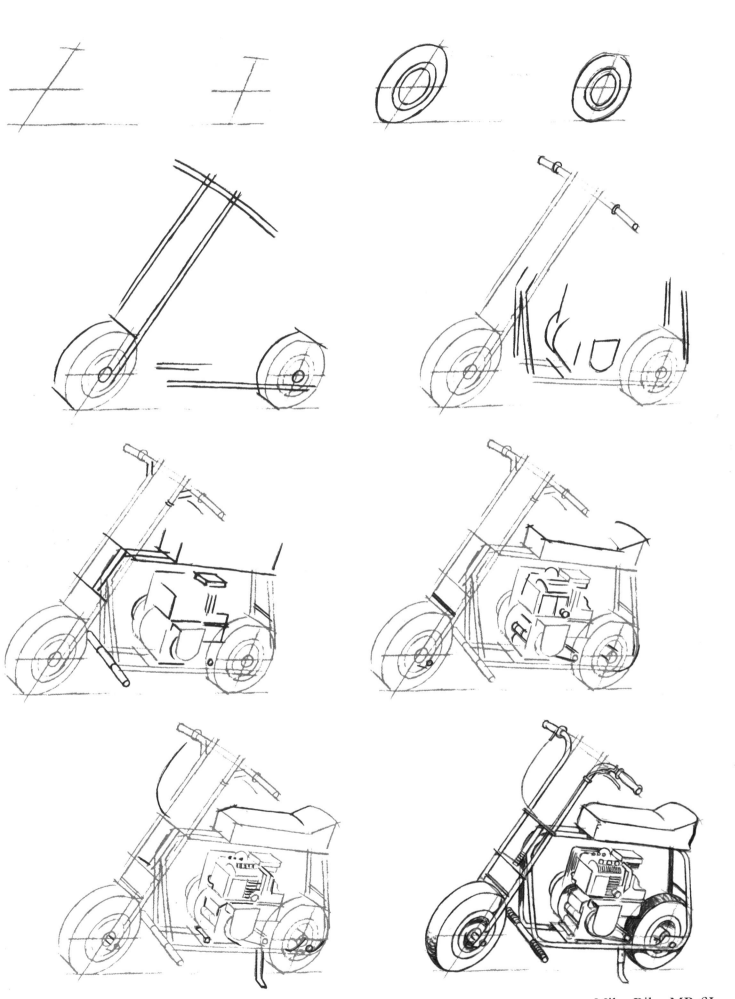

Mike-Bike MB-6L

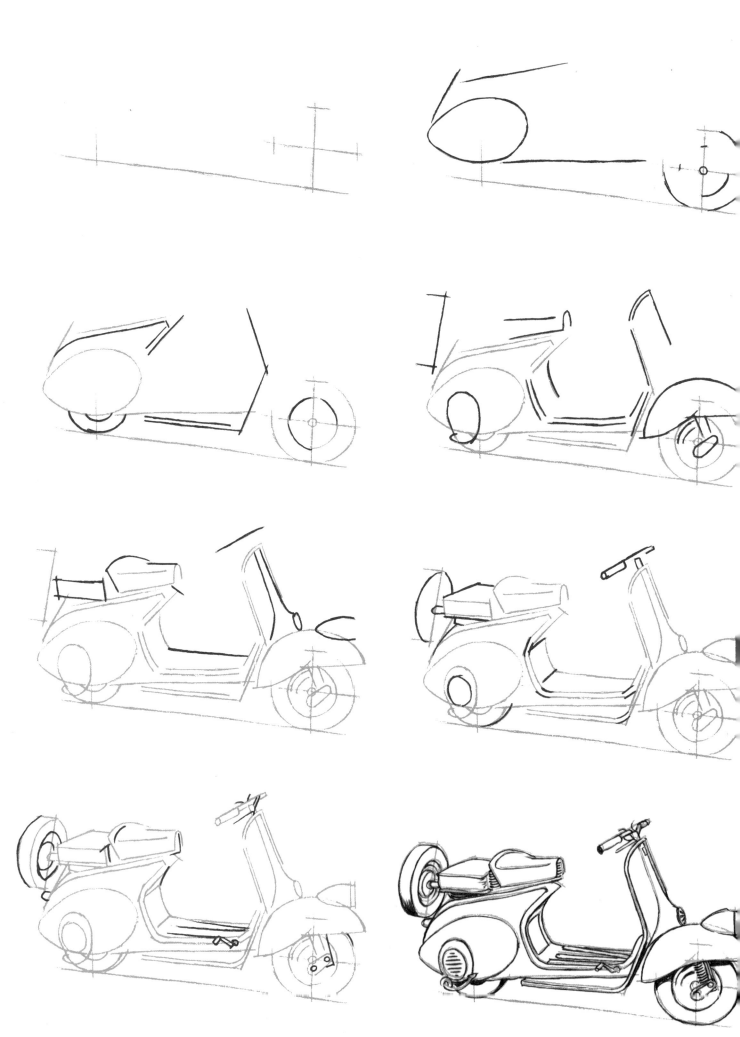

1949 Piaggio Vespa

Mini Chopper

BMW R 100RS

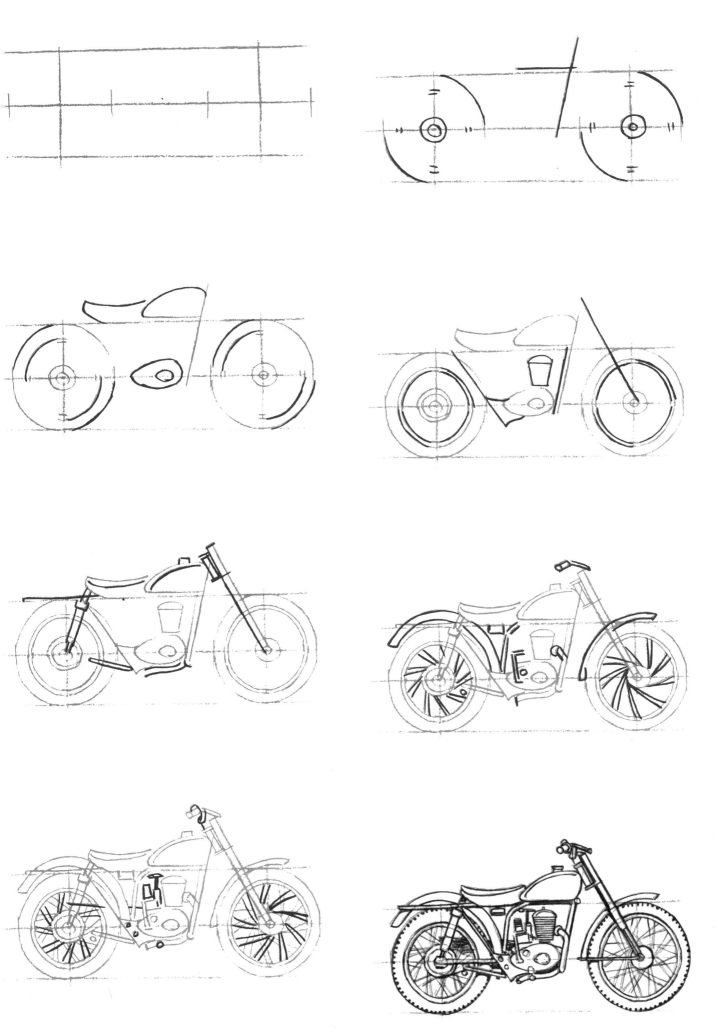

Francis-Barnett 249-c.c. Scrambler

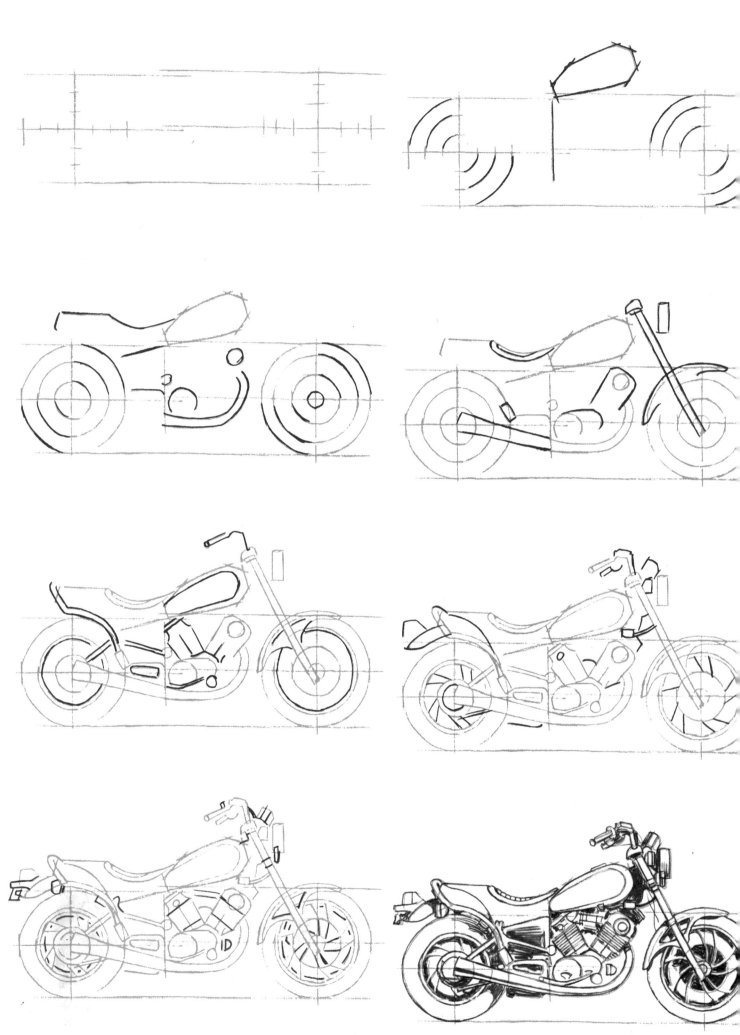

Yamaha Virago

Harley-Davidson XLH 883 Sportster

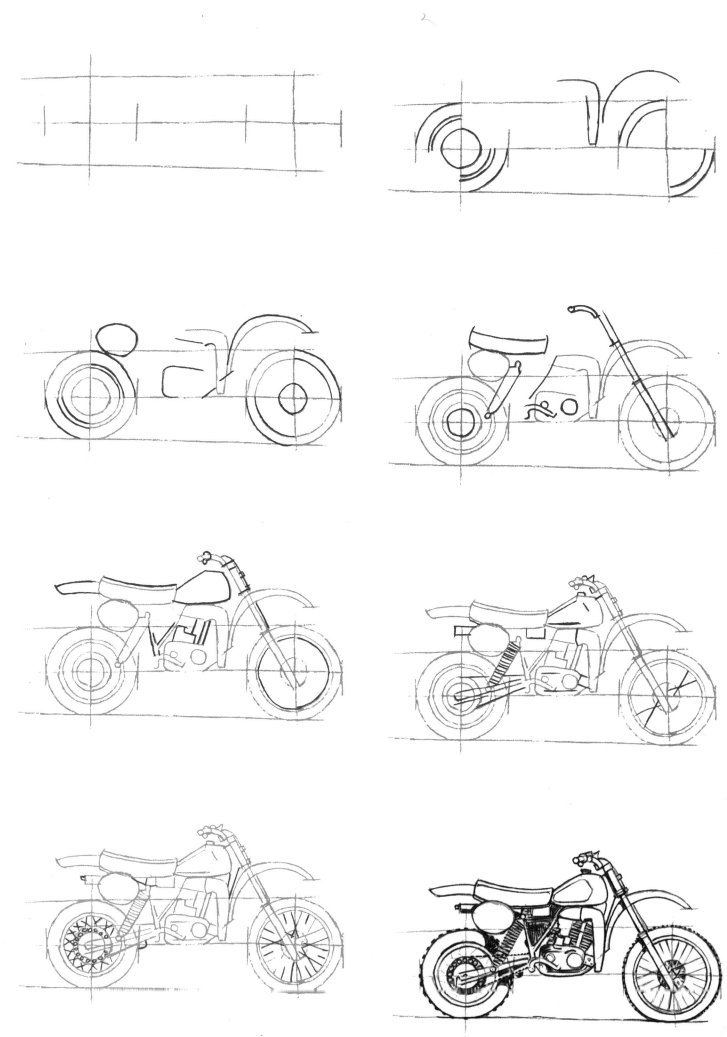

Husqvarna 430 CR

B. F. Meyers Manx 2 Dune Buggy

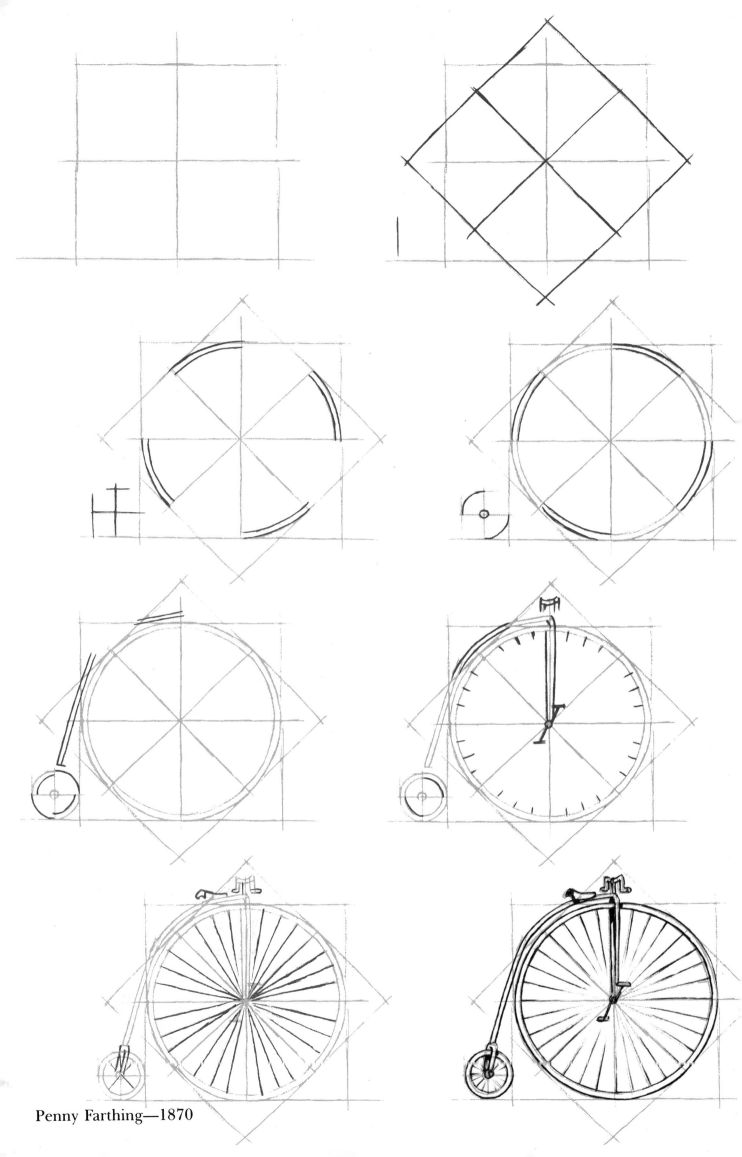

Penny Farthing—1870

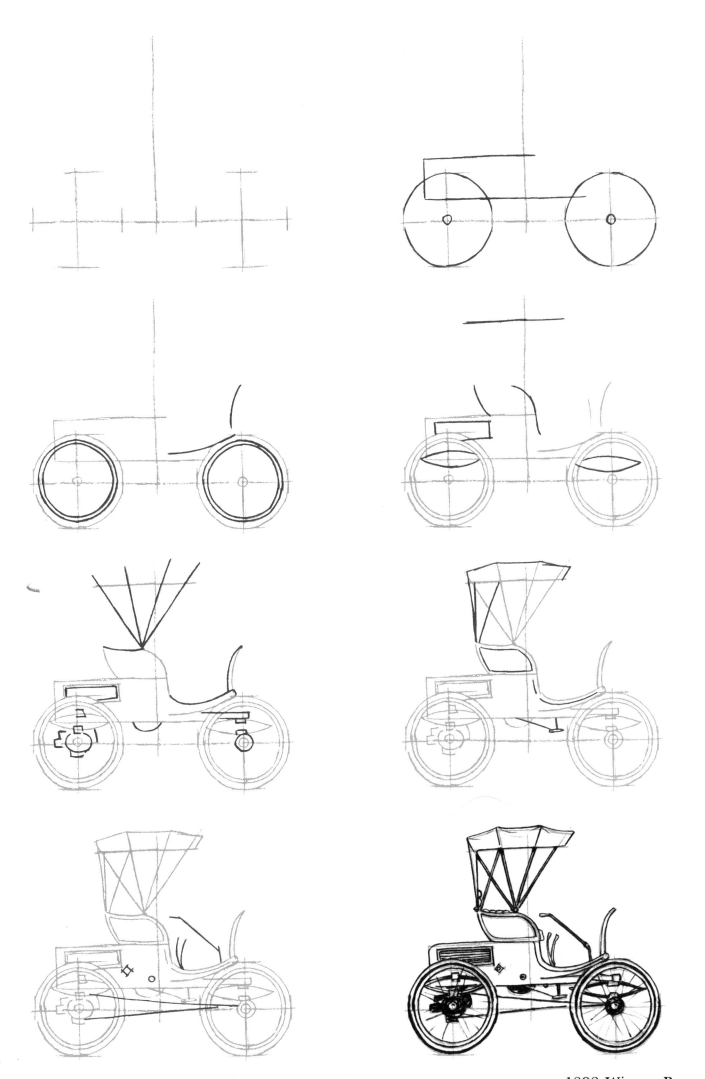

1898 Winton Buggy

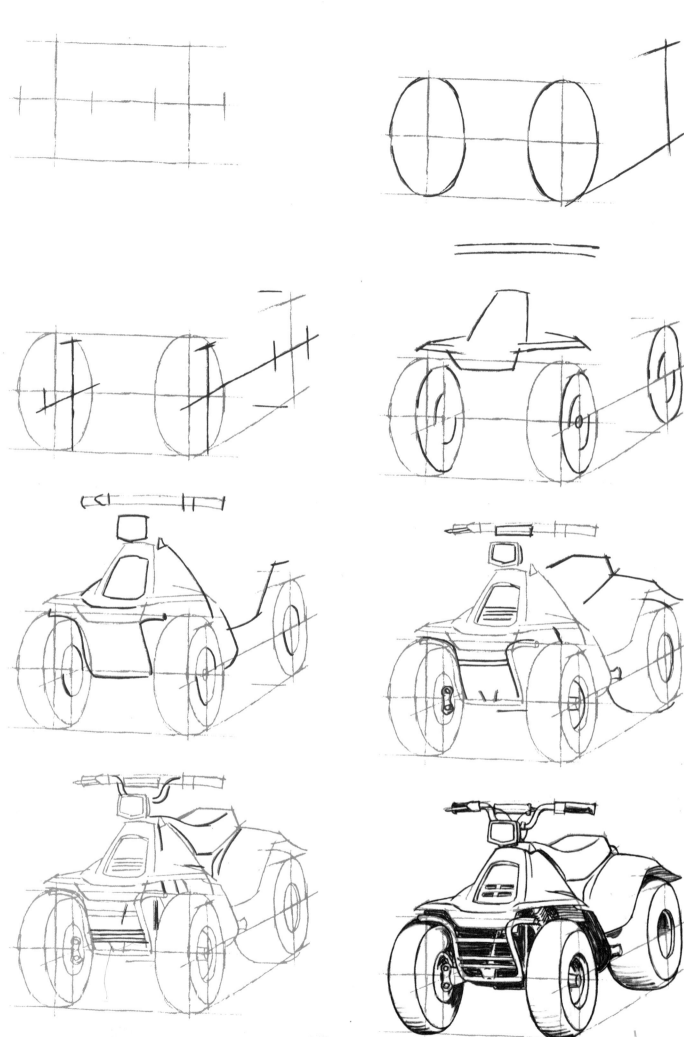

Suzuki Quadrunner 125

LEE J. AMES has been earning his living as an artist for forty-five years. He began his career working on Walt Disney's *Fantasia* and *Pinocchio*. He has taught at the School of Visual Arts in Manhattan and, more recently, at Dowling College on Long Island. He was for a time director of his own advertising agency and illustrator for several magazines. Mr. Ames has illustrated over 150 books, from preschool picture books to postgraduate texts. When not working, he battles on the tennis court. A native New Yorker, Lee J. Ames lives in Dix Hills, Long Island, with his wife, Jocelyn, their two dogs, and a calico cat.

DRAW 50 FOR HOURS OF FUN!

*Using Lee J. Ames's proven, step-by-step method of drawing instruction you can easily
learn to draw animals, monsters, airplanes, cars, sharks, buildings, dinosaurs, famous cartoons, and so much
more! Millions of people have learned to draw by using the award-winning
"Draw 50" technique. Now you can too!*

COLLECT THE ENTIRE DRAW 50 SERIES!

*The Draw 50 Series books are available from your local bookstore.
You may also order direct (make a copy of this form to order).*

Titles are paperback, unless otherwise indicated.

ISBN	TITLE	PRICE	QTY	TOTAL
23629-8	Airplanes, Aircraft, and Spacecraft	$8.95/$11.95 Can	X ———	= ———
19519-2	Animals	$8.95/$11.95 Can	X ———	= ———
24638-2	Athletes	$8.95/$11.95 Can	X ———	= ———
26767-3	Beasties and Yugglies and Turnover Uglies and Things That Go Bump in the Night	$8.95/$11.95 Can	X ———	= ———
23630-1	Boats, Ships, Trucks and Trains	$8.95/$11.95 Can	X ———	= ———
41777-2	Buildings and Other Structures	$8.95/$11.95 Can	X ———	= ———
24639-0	Cars, Trucks, and Motorcycles	$8.95/$11.95 Can	X ———	= ———
24640-4	Cats	$8.95/$11.95 Can	X ———	= ———
42449-3	Creepy Crawlies	$8.95/$11.95 Can	X ———	= ———
19520-6	Dinosaurs and Other Prehistoric Animals	$8.95/$11.95 Can	X ———	= ———
23431-7	Dogs	$8.95/$11.95 Can	X ———	= ———
46985-3	Endangered Animals	$8.95/$11.95 Can	X ———	= ———
19521-4	Famous Cartoons	$8.95/$11.95 Can	X ———	= ———
23432-5	Famous Faces	$8.95/$11.95 Can	X ———	= ———
47150-5	Flowers, Trees, and Other Plants	$8.95/$11.95 Can	X ———	= ———
26770-3	Holiday Decorations	$8.95/$11.95 Can	X ———	= ———
17642-2	Horses	$8.95/$11.95 Can	X ———	= ———
17639-2	Monsters	$8.95/$11.95 Can	X ———	= ———
41194-4	People	$8.95/$11.95 Can	X ———	= ———
47162-9	People of the Bible	$8.95/$11.95 Can	X ———	= ———
47005-3	People of the Bible (hardcover)	$13.95/$19.95 Can	X ———	= ———
26768-1	Sharks, Whales, and Other Sea Creatures	$8.95/$11.95 Can	X ———	= ———
14154-8	Vehicles	$8.95/$11.95 Can	X ———	= ———
	Shipping and handling	**(add $2.50 per order)**	X ———	= ———
		TOTAL		———

Please send me the title(s) I have indicated above. I am enclosing $_____.
Send check or money order in U.S. funds only (no C.O.D.s or cash, please). Make check payable to
Doubleday Consumer Services. Allow 4 - 6 weeks for delivery.
Prices and availability are subject to change without notice.

Name:_____

Address:_____ Apt. # _____

City:_____ State:_____ ZIP Code: _____

Send completed coupon and payment to:

Doubleday Consumer Services
Dept LA 16
2451 South Wolf Road
Des Plaines, IL 60018

MAIN STREET BOOKS

LA 16-7/96